get into

# BAKING

delicious recipes to make and taste!

katie marshall

WAYLAND

# CONTENTS

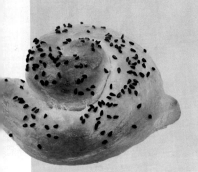

# GETTING STARTED

Whether it's cupcakes, traybakes or bread, there's nothing more exciting than sharing a homemade snack. And after the hard work of baking them, you definitely deserve a treat!

Baking is easy as pie (and just as tasty) once you know how. This book carefully explains the main baking techniques, then gives you step-by-step instructions to complete 10 delicious recipes; each one will help you master different skills.

**Dairy-free**

**Egg-free**

**Gluten-free**

There are gluten-, dairy- and egg-free options included, and we've made these recipes easy to spot with special symbols. (Some people can't eat certain ingredients, so you should always check for any allergies before offering your goodies.)

Before you get stuck into each recipe, remember to wash your hands and put on an apron. Read all the instructions through first, so you'll know exactly what you need to do. Once that's done, carefully measure out all your ingredients. Then you'll be ready to bake!

# ESSENTIAL EQUIPMENT

There are a few things you should have in your kitchen to make sure you're ready to bake.

All the temperatures listed in this book are for a conventional oven. Reduce them by 10–20 °C for fan-assisted ovens.

**APRON** Wear this to stop your clothes getting mucky!

**MEASURING JUG** A jug with measurements on it so you can judge how much liquid is inside.

**SPOONS** Use big plastic or wooden spoons for mixing ingredients. Measuring spoons help you to prepare small amounts of ingredients.

**BOWLS** It's useful to have bowls in a few different sizes. They hold your ingredients, or you can use them to mix ingredients together.

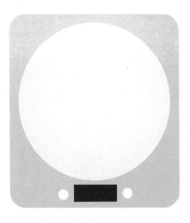

**KITCHEN SCALES** It's important to check the weight of your ingredients so you can be sure you're putting the right amounts into your bakes.

**SIEVE** A wire mesh to get rid of lumps from powders or liquids.

**BAKING PARCHMENT** This special paper, sometimes known as greaseproof paper, stops bakes from sticking to your trays and tins.

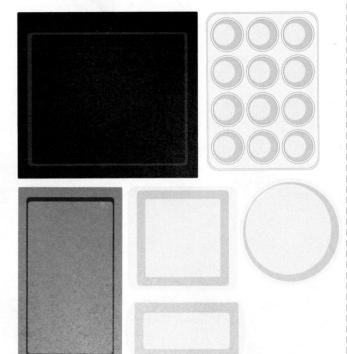

**OVEN GLOVES** These are a must whenever you're getting things out of the oven. They protect your hands from hot trays and tins.

**BAKING TRAYS AND TINS** These metal containers help bakes cook by conducting an oven's heat, and also help bakes keep their shape.

**TIMER** Use one of these to make sure your bakes will be cooked perfectly.

**WIRE RACK** It's important to cool some bakes out of the tins they were cooked in so they don't go soggy.

**PASTRY OR COOKIE CUTTERS** Cut pastry or dough into fun shapes!

# BAKING TECHNIQUES

Baking involves some key skills. Here are the most important ones:

**GREASING** It's important to put a small amount of oil or butter on the inside of a baking tin with a brush or some kitchen paper. This stops your bakes from sticking to the tin.

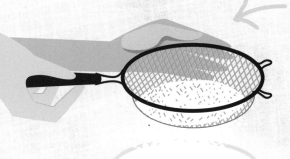

**SIFTING** Putting flour or other dry ingredients through a sieve gets rid of lumps, and gets air into your bakes to help them rise.

**CREAMING** The back of a wooden spoon is just right for smoothly blending butter and sugar together against the side of a bowl.

**RUBBING IN** Rub flour and a fat, like butter, between you fingertips. The mixture will look just like breadcrumbs when you're finished.

**MIXING** The easiest way to combine ingredients is to stir them together in a bowl using a spoon.

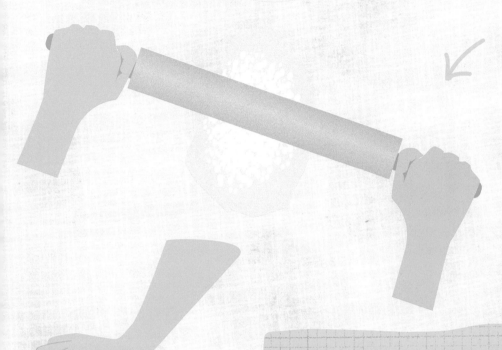

**ROLLING** To flatten out dough or pastry, sprinkle some flour on to a flat surface, then place your dough on top. Roll a rolling pin over the dough in every different direction to flatten it.

**KNEADING** This process involves stretching and folding dough with the heels of your hands. It spreads an ingredient called yeast through the dough and wakes up something called gluten, which gives many baked goods their structure.

## TESTING IF A CAKE OR BREAD IS READY

It's important not to open the oven door when you're baking as it might stop things rising. Each recipe will give you a range of cooking time, such as '20–25 minutes'. When your cake or bread has cooked for the smaller amount of time, it's safe to open the oven to test it.

**CAKE** Put a skewer into the centre of the cake. If it comes out clean, the cake is ready. If not, bake for five more minutes, then check again.

**BREAD** The bread should look golden. Carefully lift it up with a tea-towel and tap the bottom. It will sound hollow if it is completely cooked.

# SIMPLE CUPCAKES

These scrummy cupcakes are both super-easy to make and a good way to master the basics of baking. Get a wooden spoon out and you'll be ready to mix!

Makes 12 cupcakes

## YOU WILL NEED

130 g caster sugar

2 large eggs

130 g soft, unsalted butter

130 g self-raising flour

1 tsp vanilla extract

2 tbsp milk

## STEP 1

Preheat your oven to 180 °C. Put 12 muffin cases into the holes of a muffin tray.

## STEP 2

Cream the butter and sugar in a large bowl using a wooden spoon.

## STEP 3

Combine the eggs and vanilla extract in a small bowl. Add them to the butter and sugar, then mix it all together.

## STEP 4

Sift the flour into the mixture, then add the milk. Combine it all with your spoon.

## STEP 5

Carefully spoon the mixture into the 12 cases.

## STEP 6

Bake for 18–20 minutes. Cool for 10 minutes in the tray, then carefully move the cupcakes to a cooling rack. Decorate with your choice of icing.

Turn to pages 28–29 for icing recipes and decoration tips!

## ZESTY TWIST

Add a lemony kick to your cakes by replacing the milk and vanilla extract with the zest of a lemon and 2 tbsp of lemon juice.

# SHORTBREAD

You only need three ingredients for these buttery shortbread biscuits – and you can make them into any shape you want!

Makes 8–10 biscuits

 EGG-FREE

## YOU WILL NEED

65 g caster sugar, plus a little extra

130 g soft, unsalted butter

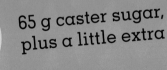

200 g plain flour, plus a little extra

## STEP 1

Preheat the oven to 180 °C and line a large baking tray with baking parchment.

## STEP 2

In a medium-sized bowl, use a wooden spoon to mix together the butter and sugar.

## STEP 3

Sift the flour into the mixture and use the spoon to mix it into the sugar and butter (it might take a little while to get it all to stick together).

## STEP 4

Sprinkle a little flour on a counter, then flatten the dough with a rolling pin until it is 1 cm thick.

The flour stops your dough from sticking to the counter.

## STEP 5

Cut out shortbread shapes using whichever cookie cutters you like.

## STEP 6

Transfer the shapes on to your baking tray and sprinkle with a little extra caster sugar. Put the tray in the fridge for 20 minutes to make the butter harden, then bake for 15–20 minutes until slightly golden. Leave plain, or decorate with icing.

## HANG 'EM UP

While they're still warm, using a chopstick, carefully make a hole in the top of each shape. When they are cool, thread string through the holes and hang them up.

# FRUIT SCONES

Mix up a batch of scones for a simple teatime treat, then eat them with jam and a dollop of whipped cream.

Makes 6–8 scones

## STEP 1
Preheat the oven to 220 °C. Line a baking tray with baking parchment. Sift the flour into a large bowl.

## STEP 2
Add the butter to the flour and rub it together with your fingertips. Add the sugar, salt and dried fruit.

## STEP 3
Pour in the milk and stir with a spoon until it all sticks together.

## YOU WILL NEED

250 g self-raising flour, plus a little extra

150 ml semi-skimmed milk, plus extra for brushing

30 g caster sugar

70 g mixed dried fruit

65 g cold, unsalted butter, chopped into cubes

½ tsp salt

## STEP 5

Cut out 6–8 circles using a 7-cm pastry cutter.

## STEP 4

Tip the dough on to a lightly floured surface and flatten to make a 2-cm-thick disc.

Squeeze the leftover dough scraps together and flatten again to make the last few scones.

## STEP 6

Pop the scones on to your baking tray, spread a little milk on the tops (either with a pastry brush or your finger) and cook for 14–16 minutes.

## EASY CHEESY

For a savoury version, leave out the sugar and dried fruit. Add 100 g of grated cheddar cheese instead.

# BANANA BREAD

This scrummy loaf is a great way to use up ripe bananas that look past their best.

Makes 1 loaf

## YOU WILL NEED

200 g self-raising flour

180 g soft, light brown sugar

200 g soft, unsalted butter

1 tsp salt

1 tsp baking powder

2–3 very ripe bananas

3 medium eggs

1 tsp vanilla extract

## STEP 1

Preheat the oven to 180 °C. Grease the inside of a 900-g loaf-tin and line it with baking parchment.

## STEP 2

In a large bowl, cream together the butter and sugar.

## STEP 3

In a separate bowl, mash the peeled bananas with the back of a fork until they look like a purée.

## STEP 4
Add the mashed banana, eggs and vanilla extract to the sugar and butter, then stir together with a wooden spoon.

## STEP 5
Sift the flour and baking powder into the bowl, add the salt, then mix it all together.

## STEP 6
Spoon the mixture into your tin and bake for between 55 minutes and 1 hour, until cooked.

# CHOC CHIP SURPRISE

Add a little extra to your loaf by popping 100 g of chocolate chips in with the flour. Double yum!

# GOOEY FLAPJACKS

Flapjacks are a great all-round treat, whether you like them oaty or nutty!

Makes 16 squares

 **GLUTEN-FREE**

## YOU WILL NEED

250 g gluten-free oats

150 g soft, light brown sugar

150 g unsalted butter

50 g golden syrup

### STEP 1
Preheat the oven to 160 °C and grease a 20-cm square tin.

### STEP 2
Put the sugar, butter and golden syrup into a saucepan and carefully melt them on the hob over a medium heat.

### STEP 3
Remove your pan from the heat and add the oats. Stir together with a wooden spoon.

## STEP 4

Pour the mixture into your tin and push down with the back of the spoon to make it all stick together.

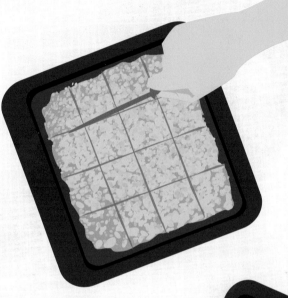

## STEP 5

Bake the mixture for 25–30 minutes until golden. Remove it from the oven and cut into 16 squares while it's still warm in the tin.

Cook the flapjacks for 5 minutes more if you like them to be crisp!

## STEP 6

When the flapjacks are completely cool, cut the squares again and carefully remove to a biscuit tin.

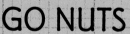

## GO NUTS

Only use 200 g oats and add them to the pan with 40 g of desiccated coconut and 60 g of mixed chopped nuts.

# PEANUT-BUTTER COOKIES

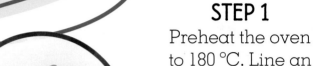

These classic American snacks are perfect for showing off to your friends (and they only take five minutes to prepare!).

Makes 24 cookies

## STEP 1
Preheat the oven to 180 °C. Line an oven tray with baking parchment

## STEP 2
In a large bowl, use a wooden spoon to mix the peanut butter and butter. Add both different types of sugar and mix together.

## YOU WILL NEED

1 medium egg

100 g soft, unsalted butter

50 g granulated sugar

150 g soft light brown sugar

½ tsp salt

¾ tsp bicarbonate of soda

½ tsp baking powder

190 g plain flour, plus a little extra

140 g peanut butter

## STEP 3
Add the egg, then sift in the plain flour, baking powder, bicarbonate of soda and salt. Stir it all until mixed together

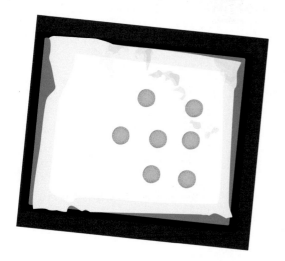

### STEP 4

Shape half the mixture into 12 ping-pong-sized balls and space out on your baking tray.

### STEP 5

Dip a fork in flour, then squash each ball of cookie dough down, making a criss-cross on top.

### STEP 6

Bake for 12–15 minutes until golden but still quite soft. Cool on the tray for 5 minutes, then carefully transfer to a wire rack. Repeat with the rest of the dough.

## JAM THUMBPRINTS

Jazz up your cookies by making a thumbprint over the criss-cross before they are baked. After cooking, when the cookies have cooled slightly, press the thumb mark with a teaspoon and fill the dip with jam.

# CARROT CAKE

Carrot? In a cake? Sounds strange … but tastes great and keeps the cake perfectly soft!

Makes 16 squares

🚫 **DAIRY-FREE**

## YOU WILL NEED

80 ml sunflower oil

150 g soft, light brown sugar

2 medium eggs

180 g carrots (about 2)

1 tsp baking powder

1 tsp bicarbonate of soda

1 tsp cinnamon

1 pinch salt

25 g plain flour

1 pinch ground ginger

## STEP 1
Lightly grease a 20-cm tin and line it with baking parchment. Preheat the oven to 180 °C.

## STEP 2
In a large bowl, mix together the flour, sugar, baking powder, bicarbonate of soda, cinnamon, ginger and salt. Break up any sugar lumps with your fingertips.

## STEP 3
Peel the skin from the carrots, then grate them and add to the bowl.

## STEP 4
In a jug, mix together the oil and eggs with a fork.

## STEP 5
Add the oil and eggs to the bowl and mix well.

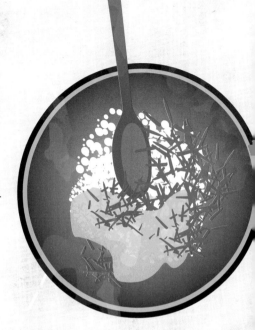

## STEP 6
Pour the mixture into the tin and bake for 30–35 minutes, until cooked. Cut into squares and enjoy plain, or top with icing.

# ONE FOR ME, ONE FOR YOU

If you fancy individual cakes instead, place 10 muffin cases in a muffin tray and divide your mixture between them. Bake for 20–25 minutes.

# SNAIL BREAD ROLLS

These rolls will teach you all you need to know about kneading – and they're shaped like little snails just for fun!

Makes 6 rolls

## YOU WILL NEED

250 g strong white bread flour, plus a little extra

1 tsp salt

1 tsp caster sugar

150 ml warm water

7-g sachet of fast-action yeast

YEAST

1 egg, beaten with a fork

### STEP 1
Preheat the oven to 220 °C. Line a baking tray with baking parchment.

### STEP 2
Put the flour, sugar, salt and yeast in a large bowl and mix together. Make a dip in the centre with a spoon.

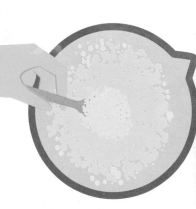

### STEP 3
Pour the water into the dip and combine the flour mixture with the water using a spoon.

## STEP 4

Tip the dough on to a lightly floured surface. Push it away from you with the heel of your left hand, then fold it back on itself. Push it away from you with your right hand, then fold it back. Repeat for 8–10 minutes until the dough is stretchy.

If your arms get tired, you might want to share the kneading with an adult!

## STEP 5

Divide the dough into six pieces and roll each one into a long sausage. Coil the sausage round to make a snail shape, with its head poking out, and pinch the back end to make a little tail.

## STEP 6

Place the snails on the baking tray and cover with cling film that has been lightly brushed with oil on the bottom. Leave to rise somewhere warm (like an airing cupboard, or near a radiator) for 30–45 minutes, until nearly doubled in size. Remove the cling film, brush with beaten egg and bake the rolls for 20–22 minutes.

# ADD SOME CRUNCH

Make your rolls more exciting by sprinkling their tops with poppy or sesame seeds before baking.

# PIZZA TWISTS

Now you've got your head around bread, it's time to have your own pizza party – with a twist ...

Makes 8 twists

 **EGG-FREE**

## YOU WILL NEED

2 tbsp tomato purée

250 g strong white bread flour, plus a little extra

1 tsp dried oregano

150 ml warm water

40 g grated Cheddar

7-g sachet of fast action yeast

1 tsp caster sugar

1 tsp salt

### STEP 1
Preheat the oven to 220 °C. Line a large baking tray with baking parchment. Make a batch of basic dough by following pages 22–23 up to Step 4. Pop the dough in a bowl, cover it with oiled cling film and leave it to rise somewhere warm for 30–35 minutes.

### STEP 2
Sprinkle a little flour on a counter and carefully stretch the dough out till it is just smaller than a sheet of A4 paper.

### STEP 3
Spread the tomato purée all over the dough to the edges.

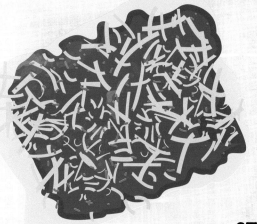

## STEP 4
Sprinkle most of the cheese and all of the oregano over the tomato.

## STEP 5
Carefully cut the dough into 8 strips with a sharp knife.

## STEP 6
Move the strips to the baking tray and twist each one a few times. Sprinkle with the rest of the cheese and bake for 14–16 minutes.

## MAKE IT GREEN
For a super-herby option, use green pesto instead of tomato purée and top it with crumbled feta instead of Cheddar.

# CHOCOLATE CAKE

This recipe is a piece of cake – tasty on a Sunday afternoon or dressed up for a birthday party.

Makes 1 large cake

## YOU WILL NEED

225 g soft, light brown sugar

200 g self-raising flour

225 g soft, unsalted butter

1 tsp salt

1 tsp baking powder

4 medium eggs

75 ml milk

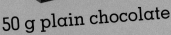

50 g plain chocolate

50 g cocoa powder

### STEP 1
Preheat the oven to 180 °C Grease two 20-cm round cake tins and line their bases with baking parchment.

### STEP 2
In a large bowl, use a wooden spoon to mix the butter and sugar together.

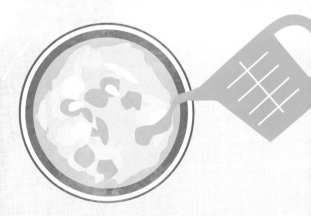

### STEP 3
Beat the eggs in a jug and pour them into the large bowl along with 1 tbsp of the flour. Mix well.

## STEP 4

Carefully melt the chocolate: ask an adult to help you to melt it either in the microwave or in a heatproof bowl over a pan of simmering water. Set it aside to cool slightly.

## STEP 5

Sift the flour, cocoa, baking powder and salt into the large bowl, then stir in the melted chocolate and milk. Mix it all together. Divide the mixture between both tins and smooth the tops. Bake for 20–25 minutes until firm to the touch.

## STEP 6

Leave the cakes in their tins for 10 minutes, then turn them out on to wire racks to cool completely. To decorate, make a double quantity of the chocolate icing on page 29. Spread one-third of the icing over the surface of one cake and put the second cake on top. Cover the sandwich cake with the rest of the icing and add sweets on top.

## MIX IT UP

Try covering the assembled cake with vanilla icing instead, and decorate the top with sweets.

# ICING AND DECORATING

Your cakes and biscuits will be a treat on their own, but you can add colour and something special by finishing them off with icing and decorations.

## BASIC VANILLA ICING

Enough for 12 cupcakes. Double the quantities to decorate the cake on pages 26–27.

In a large bowl, use a wooden spoon to beat 120 g of soft butter. Sift in 150 g of icing sugar and mix until combined. Then add another 150 g of icing sugar, 2 tbsp of milk and 2 tsp of vanilla extract, and mix until smooth. Use a balloon whisk near the end to make the icing even fluffier.

You can add a couple of drops of food colouring to your vanilla icing to make it more exciting.

# CHOCOLATE ICING

**Enough for 12 cupcakes. Double the quantities to decorate the cake on pages 26–27.**

Follow the vanilla icing recipe, but when you add the second batch of icing sugar, only sift in 110 g. At the same time, add 40 g of cocoa powder.

Writing icing and colourful sprinkles, available in most supermarkets, are perfect for decorating cakes, biscuits and cookies. If you want to make something super-special, why not add chocolate buttons, grated chocolate, Smarties, mini-marshmallows or even edible glitter!

You can make either icing dairy-free by using lacto-free milk, dairy-free spread instead of butter and dairy-free cocoa powder.

# ALLERGIES AND INTOLERANCES

Some people suffer from allergies that make their bodies react badly to certain types of food – even a small trace can make them extremely ill. Other people might not be allergic, but may have an intolerance. That means they have difficulty digesting certain types of food, but their reaction is not as severe as that of an allergy.

Gluten, dairy, eggs and nuts are the main substances in this book that people might be allergic to. When baking for friends and family, check for any allergies before you start cooking. We've highlighted recipes that avoid certain food types, but it's often possible to swap tricky ingredients for special ones that are allergen-free.

Nowadays, there are lots of **dairy-free** alternatives, such as soya milk, almond milk and vegetable-oil spreads (to use instead of butter). Some of these will add a slightly different flavour to your baking, and might affect the look or texture, but should make a dairy recipe suitable for someone who is allergic.

**Eggs** do lots of important things in baking. It might be safer to stick to egg-free breads if you have guests with egg allergies, but if you really want to try a recipe that includes eggs, look on the internet to find out about egg substitutes.

**Gluten** plays an important part in some bakes, so it's not always possible to have a gluten-free option. You can replace self-raising flour with gluten-free self-raising flour, but the results may vary. You can also buy gluten-free baking powder.

# GLOSSARY

**ALLERGEN** Something that can cause somebody to have an allergic reaction.

**BALLOON WHISK** A stirring tool designed to get air into a mixture.

**BEAT** To mix or stir ingredients together until they're combined.

**BICARBONATE OF SODA** A white powder that reacts with other ingredients in baking to make things rise.

**CHOPSTICK** One of two pointed sticks, often used to eat Asian food.

**CONDUCT** To transfer heat.

**DAIRY** Describes something made from cow's milk.

**DESICCATED** Something dried out, intentionally, to stop it going bad. This changes the texture and flavour.

**FOOD COLOURING** A liquid or gel that can add extra, or unusual, colour to food.

**GLUTEN** A protein found in wheat and other grains. It allows dough to stretch.

**GRANULATED** Describes little crystals of sugar.

**LACTO-FREE** Describes products that don't contain dairy.

**PURÉE** Cooked food that has been blended.

**SAVOURY** Food that isn't sweet, such as bread.

**SELF-RAISING FLOUR** A type of flour that has special ingredients to help bakes rise.

**SKEWER** A long piece of metal or wood with a sharp point, used in cooking.

**YEAST** An ingredient used to make bread rise.

**ZEST** The skin of citrus fruits – it has a strong flavour.

# INDEX

Published in Great Britain in 2018 by Wayland

Copyright © Wayland, 2016

All rights reserved.

Editor: Liza Miller
Designer: Simon Daley
Illustration: Ana Djordjevic
Photography: Simon Pask

ISBN: 978 15263 0049 2

10 9 8 7 6 5 4 3 2 1

Wayland
An imprint of
Hachette Children's Group
Part of Hodder & Stoughton
Carmelite House
50 Victoria Embankment
London EC4Y 0DZ

An Hachette UK Company
www.hachette.co.uk
www.hachettechildrens.co.uk

Printed in China

The website addresses (URLs) included in this book were valid at the time of going to press. However, it is possible that contents or addresses may have changed since the publication of this book. No responsibility for any such changes can be accepted by either the author or the Publisher.

The Publisher would like to thank the following for permission to reproduce their pictures. Via Shutterstock: p 9r aquariagirl1970; p 15r Michal Zduniak; p 17l Elena Veselova